:

Defeating Demons:

Journey thru Poetry

Wanda Bigler
Wanda Jackson

Table of Contents: Poems

Happy Birthday, llisha
Having loved someone so much
Jesus is my Lord and Savior
Time to get right
True Wealth
Intimacy
We Use to be in Love
Christ Like
Thank you Lord
Concentrate on Me
Marry me today
Lips are sealed
My Chocolate Thunder
My Ultimate Goal
My Own Dreams
Petrifying Chatter
Endeavor
Bright and Shining Star
Brings me death
I love you
Its suicide
I've already died
Kindness in your soul
Insincere price
In the World
In the first place
Who am I: Human Being?

Life
To be your wife
Body Freeze
Cherish friendship forever
Working my nerves
Work of art
Wish
Willing to lose
Whose fighting who
Who belongs together?
When you fall
When I say I love you
What you didn't do all along
No longer feeling me
Ain't Nobody Equipped
All my need
Funeral broke
Empty and Scampered
How l once was
Letting go
You're not listening
I'll Miss
I'll always love you
My Chocolate Thunder
My Ultimate Goal
My Own Dreams
What I'm Seeking

Dedication

I'd like to first give Thanks to my Lord and Savior Jesus Christ who died for my sins and also in whom I dedicate this book, as well as, dedication to my sweet husband Christopher Bigler, my mama Debra F. Jackson, my dad William Jackson Sr., my brother William Jackson Jr., my brother Wayne Jackson, my grandma Frances Fairchild, all of those who are now deceased: humans & pets, my sister & brother from another mister Jason and Monica Blakley, my best friends Joseph and Nina Baleta, my godson Jaiden Baleta, my Godchildren Amarra Guess and Summer Elizabeth and their beloved-deceased mother, my dear friend Amelia Guess and their father Randell Guess, my uncle and auntie Michael and Candace, my adopted family: Tami Radohl-Sigley, Matt Sigley & their children H, M, and Ty. family, my adopted family: The Diekemper Family, my adopted family: Gary and Julie, all of my extended family (blood relatives; The Jackson Family, the Fairchild Family, The Thompson Family, The Horne Family, adopted relatives, and in-laws The Bigler Family), all of my cousins, aunts, uncles, adopted nephews and nieces, my adopted families(s); The Hamilton Family, the Norise Family, The Trotter family, the Sutton Family, and the Tyse Family, my adopted nana Tina H-Baker, my adopted sister Jennifer Moats, my Facebook family and friends, all of my K-12 teachers @ Point Elementary, Oakville Middle School, and Oakville Senior High school, all of my college professors @ Missouri State University & Park University, my dear friends Sarah Wright, Michele Rutayuga, Michelle Marrant, my Salvation Army Family, Great Circle family, all of my current employers, family, and colleagues in Missouri & Kansas, those who bullied me and conspired against me, and my enemies, all the churches that I have attended & church family that I obtained in the process, all of my children both living and dead, and everyone who has crossed paths with me in this life and the next.

A special thanks to Jon Jorgensen. I do not know you and have never met you, but you have inspired me to step outside my shell and do something I have never done. My poem: "Out of his hands" was inspired by your spoken word "A Godless Generation". This was the first poem I spoke at a Poetry Slam on an open mic night. This was the first time I'd ever done an open mic night. It was both scary and liberating.

Please hold any forgotten mentions to my head and not my heart. I Love You all.

Foreword

The reason for this book is to share intimate moments of trials and tribulations, struggles with mental illness, love, suicidal thoughts and attempts, depression, success, fear, hopefulness, hopelessness, sex, Christianity, Spirituality, and other parts of my life's journey in poetry form in hope that it can inspire other's who may be battling the same thing. If I don't leave this life with anything else, I hope that my words will help guide others and bring peace into this crazy world and maybe impact at least 1 life. Thank You!

Love,

Wanda Bigler
Wanda Jackson

PROLOGUE

"Out of his hands"

Inspired by "A Godless Generation" by Jon Jorgenson
https://www.youtube.com/watch?v=zng2piCy4RA

"When did the movement of Jesus begin to lose its authenticity"?

This is a line from Jorgenson's spoken word and how his words started to get to me
Listening to him speak about church in its history
Reminded me of my own struggles with Christianity and intimacy
I could blame Dunnie; I think I was about 10, that's the man that started caressing me
Or I could blame my aunt Diane who slept in the same bed while he molested me
And although I didn't tell my parents I could blame them for not rescuing me
But it was easier to blame Jesus because wasn't he supposed to be there to protect me
This poem isn't to crucify Jesus; I love him; bare with me I'm just getting started
Remember this poem is about intimacy and my addiction to playing victim and being broken hearted
To blame everyone else for what happened and leave trust up to pardon
I read in the Bible where it states to "pray without ceasing" but this I disregarded
Instead of asking God to mend what was in my heart that began to harden
You know what, that's how things all got started
I'll never forget my dad introducing me to church because without it I would have lost it
For those who wonder where God is in situations like Boston
He's at the same place where we started separating church from state and began releasing murderers who killed 9 people because he was "mentally exhausted"
But don't blame God for these tragedies even though I get some of your reasons
It's easier to blame someone we choose not to get to know daily because sins easier to believe in
Having sex with multiple men and getting shots for diseases
That was easier to do to mend the pain then to pray to someone who allowed family members to molest children
So, "When did the movement of Jesus; begin to lose its authenticity"?
When we started putting our trust in men to handle and protect things that's weren't meant for them.

26 June 2016

ISBN: 9780578677675
ISBN 978-0-578-67767-5

"Out of his hands"

Inspired by "A Godless Generation" by Jon Jorgenson
https://www.youtube.com/watch?v=zng2piCy4RA

"When did the movement of Jesus begin to lose its authenticity"?

This is a line from Jorgenson's spoken word and how his words started to get to me
Listening to him speak about church in its history
Reminded me of my own struggles with Christianity and intimacy
I could blame Dunnie; I think I was about 10, that's the man that started caressing me
Or I could blame my aunt Diane who slept in the same bed while he molested me
And although I didn't tell my parents I could blame them for not rescuing me
But it was easier to blame Jesus because wasn't he supposed to be there to protect me
This poem isn't to crucify Jesus; I love him; bare with me I'm just getting started
Remember this poem is about intimacy and my addiction to playing victim and being broken hearted
To blame everyone else for what happened and leave trust up to pardon
I read in the Bible where it states to "pray without ceasing" but this I disregarded
Instead of asking God to mend what was in my heart that began to harden
You know what, that's how things all got started
I'll never forget my dad introducing me to church because without it I would have lost it
For those who wonder where God is in situations like Boston
He's at the same place where we started separating church from state and began releasing murderers who killed 9
people because he was "mentally exhausted"
But don't blame God for these tragedies even though I get some of your reasons
It's easier to blame someone we choose not to get to know daily because sins easier to believe in
Having sex with multiple men and getting shots for diseases
That was easier to do to mend the pain then to pray to someone who allowed family members to molest children
So, "When did the movement of Jesus; begin to lose its authenticity"?
When we started putting our trust in men to handle and protect things that's weren't meant for them.

26 June 2016

This was the first poem I spoke at a Poetry Slam on an open mic night. This was
the first time I'd ever done an open mic night. It was both scary and liberating.

Give us a try

Being in a relationship made me realize something more
That I need to come closer to myself than I ever had before
I mean I don't know how I feel about me; how can I feel about someone else
I'm holding on to some sort of pain that I may have gotten somewhere else
I don't know if I'm holding on as a source to get away from it all
Or is my heart fallen short from love, is it too soon to recall?
I'm still young so it's okay not to know what I want
But that older sense to be mature comes to my thoughts as it haunts
It tells me I'm making a mistake and I'm falling in too soon
That I need to take a break that I'm falling for a fool
It makes me feel as if there's nothing out of life I should take
That I need to slow down, that I finally need that break
From what I'm not sure that's where my heart comes to play
It tells me to hold on, that it's possible to find a way
It tells me not to fall into deep because of possibilities to get hurt
But it tells me to take a risk because that's the only way it'll work
Now I've made it this far and I think I've come along way
That I have a plan in life and that I can make away
But there's just something missing I just don't know what it is
I feel love and support right now that's what I feel
I've never felt this way about anyone before
I'll never open enough for someone to walk through those doors
But maybe they've come to soon maybe too soon to early too far
I haven't had that role in my life to bring me this far
Now I've been going in separate directions and I haven't even slowed down
I haven't had the chance to think to myself or have that look around
It seems like every time there are good things there are strings attached facing down
Feelings of depression, self-consciousness, and anxiety with a frown
Am I using him to get away, am I using him as that key?
That one key to get away from that stress that's smothering me
Is he that person in life that's only for a season?
That person to bring me comfort and support and help me make sense & reason
Or is he a lifeline person that's there for me by and by
But I'm being tested to see if I can handle my own pride
I don't think I'll ever really know because of that one doubtful thought in my mi
That's the part I need to get rid of or is it some sort of sign
A sign telling me things will be OK and that I can move forward not back
A sign that tells me that I've made it on the right track
It's been a long time and now I'm starting to wonder
If there will ever be a time, I could go without my chocolate thunder
He's been there for me; he's cared for me in every single way
I know I love him, and I adore him and I'm going through a phase
It's time for me to conclude, a last thought for the mind
My mind tells me it's just a phase, my heart tells me it's a sign
After all this time and effort, I want to give us a try

Friendship

Why suffer to hold it all in, it's not hurting anyone but you
Why stay distant from the one you claim you truly love especially when they love you
It's understandable to have a flaw, but to when the flaw controls you
When it starts to break up good friendships with those who are close to you
Independence is a lovely thing, a great feeling to be who you are
It's also good to share your wealth, your happiness, and your heart
You say you understand where I'm coming from, but you don't seem to have the perspective clear just a tip
Without trust, love, and clear communication it's impossible to have a good friendship

Wanders

Doesn't make it special
On the inside; it's a lie
The negativity
The human immortality
The tears in my eyes…
The what if's
the happens
"Que Paso"
Si Si nething
Somehow some way
Has no special meaning
The thoughts
The feelings
Aren't forced
But could be real
Forced entry
Forced mentally
Feelings to be real…
There's never really been trust
But vulnerability
To be wanted
But there is still no special
Meaning
My innocence;
Still wanders…

4 May 2009

"Prayer"

Guilt and shame
But no regrets "inhale"
Lies and cheats
I dare not to re-tell
My actions are as followed
My words are as said
Memories, my actions
I dare not re-tell
What has come over me?
Why feel these sudden exhales?
Don't know what I should do
Internal decisions want to re-tell
Against my religion
Against my morals
My thoughts
My frights, my fears to pray
My sins, my faults
Decisions without knowledge
Doesn't make it my fault
But to gain knowledge of such actions
Makes my continued choices my fault
Shall they be forgiven?
Will only begin with my decision to want
My actions must stop
Love or lust
Human nature of wants
I must regain consciousness
I must begin to regain again "exhale"
My faith, my religion
Why am I scared now of this word "Prayer"?

4 May 2009

Attentively

Sitting here thinking
getting a better understanding
of how life works
not knowing but observing
don't really have to know
just have an idea
not if being wrong
knowing how you feel
writing aggressively
writing maliciously
not to be negative
but express what's there physically
still moments
clear moments
dull moments
listening
no eye contact
open ears
clear ideas
attentively

21 January 2009

Failure

We learn from what we do
We learn from what we say
This is a life lesson
As we approach them day by day
Being right is an extra
Being wrong is being brave
Writing is being expressive
Our voice used excessively
Our mind we tend to waste
Photos taken to capture
Pictures used as detail
Effort shows our most prideful moments
Our fear we hold as failure

21 January 2009

Friends Life

Attoria raced around the corner and watched her target retrieve her folders.
Attoria's target Sierra rolled her eyes, while walking away, and shrugging her shoulders.
Sierra explained to her friend next to her how she gets down in the south.
Attoria yells "yeah right" and slammed her fist to sierra's mouth.
Attoria threw her hand on sierra's weave and wrapped her hair around her fist
Standing so close to her face she could have gave her a kiss
Sierra screams, "Let go of me before I put my foot to your ass"
Her fellow students now realize what's happening and laugh as they pass
Sierra tried to get a grip on Attorias hand to set her hair free
But Attoria pulls tighter punching her not twice, but in threes
Sierra starts crying as she's being lowered closer to the floor
She tries so hard not to fall, while holding on to her shirt that's now torn
Sierra finally gets a grip on Attoria and kicks her in the chin
Sierra's friend jumps in and starts hitting her again, then again
Attoria yells. "So ya'll gotta jump me to prove a point
And ya'll aren't nothing but some scared bitches up in this joint"
Sierra screams "you the scared botch that's why you caught me off guard"
Attoria yells back "you just can't fight that why I left you a bald spot" which later turned into a scar
The friend lets Attoria go thinking she beat her enough
She starts to cuss at her like she's someone real tough
But Attoria played it smart as if she was heading back to class
She then turns around and starts beating the friend's ass
The friend realizes what's happening and tries her best to fight back
But Attoria's other friends heard the news and start giving her a brutal attack
Sierra just stands there not returning the friends favor
She lets her get beat up until there was nothing or no one there to save her
Later finding out the friend's name was Shanice was sent away on a stretcher
She ended up in a medically induced coma for several weeks and the death angels to catch her
Instead of standing there watching her friend get stabbed with a knife
She didn't have to fight again but get help to save her friends life.

Lesson: Don't be a bystander, recording and watching, stop violence while it's occurring by getting help.
This poem was written in March 2015 but is still a reality now in 2019.
#stoptheviolence

August 24, 2007

It all started in meteorology when the principal called me out of class
I was confused, did I do something wrong, was it for something in my past
I guess the look on my face was startling because my whole class reacted with comments and giggles
The principal told me I wasn't in trouble, just needed to talk to me for minute
I talk to him about possibly joining the COE program again and talking to Miss Clark later in that day
I talk to her until a little past lunch and was excited and In a way
It was just something about the day that just completely threw me off
I had a chance to be late to class; my body really relaxed and started to feel soft
But they sort of was easy-going and I begin to be called out of class a lot
When I went to my last hour, the announcement for me to come with my belongings became a real plot
The bell was going to rain in about five or six minutes so why would they want with me
Miss Hessel told me to go into the conference room and wait for the phone to ring
She said my mother was on the phone, so as I walked back, I cracked a joke for relief
But When I say hello, another voice began to speak
Wanda, this is Jasmine, I'm at the hospital, and he got hit by a truck
At this moment tears filled my eyes and I'm thinking "what the fuck? "
I'm thinking is he OK, is he gone, is he still alive
I'm thinking this can't be happening as the tears ran down my eyes
I begin to stop and pause even though I'm already standing still
My knees are weak I'm starting to shake, this can't be for real
I hear Jasmine tell me he's OK, but it's not going through my head
My thoughts are still going, oh my gosh, Tyrone please you can't be Dead
This is where I realize that Jazmin is actually talking and she's telling me what hospital they are in
She tells me St. Louis University and reassures me that he's OK
The bell rings, it seems like forever, this is way too much for one day
We talk for a second longer and I began to hang up the phone
I begin to walk outside; we are thinking about everything that could've possibly went wrong
I didn't Begin to realize until this day that life is too short to waste
That life could have been gone in an instant, so with that I think God for his love, his mercy, and Grace

Weight I

You know why it's so hard to lose weight.
Cause you spend so much time on plenty of fish; looking for a date.
But not the good guy that calls you beautiful.
Or the good guy who just says hi.
No, you want the cute guy with nappy hair.
That take pictures of your most treasure secrets the other night
The guy who has a weird smile who you'd pass up in the store
No, you want the guy who fucks you and uses you for rides and doesn't respond to your messages anymore
What about the guy who wants stimulating conversation because that's what you ask for in your profile am I correct you stupid bitch?
Nah, he's too busy spending time with child & you want the guy whose five-year plan is "getting lit".
Now you gotta go get an STD test because you let him fuck you raw.
Instead of the guy who asked you politely to take you out on a date and all he wanted to do was call.

9 May 2016

Weight II

You really wanna know it's so hard to lose weight

Cause you passed that oatmeal by on your way to burger king

You pass that fruit smoothie by on your way to some down the street

And instead of working out w/ your roommate you went to go ice cream & then went to sleep

You went to go get wing stop instead of stopping by planet fitness

You walk pass that water about 8 times just to go get those juices out the kitchen

Now you are asking God for favor because the scale say 234

But this whole time you could have been on your way to work out instead of cleaning & mopping the floor

You keep looking at that water but won't drink it, you keep writing because you have so much to say

Just don't be at this again tomorrow wondering why it's so hard to lose weight

9 May 2016

Administrative Leave

Love is supposed to be patient, Love is supposed to be kind
I know, there's goes that girl with all that church stuff in her rhymes
But this go around let's think on a more political ground
Take a step back from the Bible and begin speaking on organized crime

When we say #BLACKLIVESMATTER, that doesn't mean that other lives don't
It just means we're tired of seeing our mugshots on the media
After we're murdered in cold blood
It means we're tired of having to justify why we're so offended and how our lives matter to us
And why we keep getting attacked and our dead bodies are left out for hours to bleed
While the boys in blue get sent home on Paid Administrative Leave

Approx.: 9 May 2016

#SAYTHEIRNAMES

I saw on the news about officers in Dallas who were shot down and I couldn't say I was
surprised
At the time it wasn't the Godliest thing to project, but I have some anger built up on the inside

I said that someday people would learn how it feels to be us & maybe they would understand or
be willing
But I think it's important to note that gunning down officers to mend outrage will never stop
them from killing.

Us.

Maybe it's time to take a different approach same sound with a different hook
That 39 in the old; 27 in the New, I'm referring to the Holy Book

Protesting. Protesting.
Hands Up. Don't Shoot.
While the media makes a mockery of our Black men

So, for my Prayer warriors, "Yes, everyone" one size does fit all, when it come to him.
For where two or three are gathered in my name, there I am in the midst of them.

I will not apologize for taking this to church, I will say the name of the Lord in vain.
The protesting approach works for many folks
In my War Room:
#EricGardner
#SandraBland
#MikeBrown
#AlterSterling
#TrayvonMartin

P.S And all of those who were murdered in vain, now deceased, rest in peace
I will continue to #SAYTHEIRNAMES.

Con't to Love

You say that when times feel like they're not getting better I'm there to help you through
You say that when you know you can't, I'm there saying you can
You say you don't know why; why I continue to push & I say to have Faith and through the ups and
down. I say we are as one:

One Love
Stay Strong
Always

Well when times feel like they are getting better, I'm there to help you through because you've brought so
much joy to my life. And when you know you can't, I'm there saying: You Can because Guess What?

YOU CAN.

You always told me I could too. When you don't know why; why I continue to push, but I say to have
Faith.

I do.

Cause I believe in the Lord's will, we believe in "Life" and we understand each other.

I believe in. Us.

But through all the ups and downs, I say we are as one; I say:

We are One Love., My First & Only

Stay Strong because this is what we need to do to get by and:

ALWAYS.

"Because that's how long I'll continue to love you"

27 December 2006; 5:38pm

Letter to TH

You've always been my everything
You've been my pride & joy
You make me smile when I am depressed
You're my love, you're my all.
And even though we're friends
Our hearts are always forever.
We've shared everything, done everything
I really wish us forever
Love is one of the greatest things
And you told me that's the best thing to be enjoyed.
We've shared these thoughts, we've shared these times
I'll cherish this most of all.
I hope things are going great with you
I hope you're happy; it feels good to be free
But most of all I want you to know I love you
And promise you'll never forget about me!

Love Always,
Wanda Jackson
single again

At Graduation

I sick n tired of people lying to my face
When dey know dey ain't truthful and breathe smell like waste

Like dis one gurl for instance she only knows to lie
But when mugs don't wanna talk to her she be about to break down and cry

Whaz duh point of doing wrong when you gonna eventually get caught
What's duh point in blamin others when you know it's your fault

But I don't care no more seriously, all I care for is Christ, real friends, family, & education
While others who worry about nonchalant problems get held back, I'll be at graduation.

30 November 2004; 10:33pm

Holocaust

There once was a time in history when it wasn't about the black or white race
But the Jewish, who suffered also in a time of disgrace
Mira Ryczke and her family one of the few Jews who were persecuted & killed
All whose families and friends were tortured in concentration camps in rare open fields?
Their houses were stormed, businesses wrecked, and their own synagogues controlled
They were forced on sight to move out of their homes & to move into "ghettos"
The Holocaust was a tragedy in history that would be remembered for grief and sin
The Holocaust was a graphic horror sight that I hope would never happen again
They were hauled off on trains and forced into Auschwitz to die
Over 200,000 prisoners worked 12-hour shifts as slave laborers had to work until they cried
Even healthy individuals would work until they dropped dead of diseases, exhaustion, & malnutrition
Children were forced to work also so no time for college or need for tuition
Leon Bass, a young American soldier, described the barracks in Buchwald at the end of the war
They were built to hold 50 people, the room house more then 150 bunks build almost to the ceiling, all the way to the floor.

"Make this work"

Baby I'm not great wit sharing my emotions, but this can't wait
I don't wanna compare you to anyone, but no one has ever made me feel this way
No one has continued to say the things you say to me, unless I edge them on at their will
I appreciate all that you do, and I just want you to know, I'll always try my best to keep it real
This could be meant to be forever or just meant to be for right now
To me it doesn't matter, this is the present and we live for right now
I don't ever wanna take you for granted I just want this to be true
I've been through a lot of emotional changes, but I know like Aaliyah, that I care for you
I don't wanna live in the past, talk about it, or bring it up
This is 2008, we're together, and I wanna live for us
I don't like to make promises because I don't like people to get hurt
I just want you to know that I'm trying and I'm willing to make this work.

Sunday 13 July 2008

Crave for you

Dear R.D.M,

You say you feelin me
I'm feelin you too
You say I'm cute
And shit, I thank you

You say the beauty inside me like the beauty in nature
The grass, the trees, the leaves, they green, but shit there's no paycheck
That'll make me feel the way I feel about you see the beauty I sometimes feel I haven't seen
You've told me things, I told you things; we connect; it's all the same

You say you like my toes
I say I like yo determination
You say you like my smile
To me that's an inspiration

The way you smile at me & the way you look at me ain't nothin I've ever seen
I may have said this before, but shit I don't say something I don't mean

I'm glad you feelin me cause I'm feelin you
Like white castles, it's what you crave and baby; I crave for you!

12 July 2008

Adulthood

As I begin entering adulthood
I begin to realize how much more
important it is to gain more
knowledge
to show more resect
to inherit more maturity
to back up everything else I've ever
said, spoken, thought, or interpreted
How much more important it is
to gain a better understanding
of what it truly means to be me.
Being independent does not only mean
to not want or feel the need to take
orders from those around me
but to try and listen and
be attentive and take in all that
can be learned and restored into
something better
To pray more believe more
and have faith…
To appreciate those around me
because they are there for reasoning
and I may never know when
it/life can be taken away
at such split moments…
Take knowledge
Take consideration
Take action
Endure leadership…
/adulthood/

10 June 2009

Extraordinary Letter

Why is the world so filled with anger and violence all the time?
Silly drive-by's over jealousy probably and murder is an unlawful crime
Why not talk it out or just leave it be?
Why not take the time to listen when some emotions are hard to see?
Why be racist when you know everyone's different in their own ways
Why put someone else down just because you're having a bad day
Why have enemies when there's already enough war going on
Why not make music and sing yourself a thoughtful song?
There's no since of acting crazy just because you don't know no better
When you're having stressful times just write yourself an extraordinary letter.

29 October 2004; 7:36pm-7:38pm

We belong together

No this is not about Mariah Carey; I'm just borrowing the title
So there ain't no need to call a doctor, I maybe a lil crazy, but I'm not homicidal

That would be crazy because it's a commandment not to kill
Plus, this poem ain't about that it's about us & if this is real

I mean you have steeze, you have style, and you have so much class
And I have dignity, I have personality, and hellava fat ass

I think that's important in both of us because that can be what helps us get through any weather
Now for my favorite part, I think *sings* the end: We belong together

30 June 2005; 6:31pm
/Revised/

Time Spent with me

Like flowers in the spring and rain in May
My heart pours out for you each & everyday

From the time I worked with you in social studies; I started feeling for you
From the in between time that I wrote you; I knew those feelings were true

At that moment I realized how it would be great to have you
Even as a friend would turn me insanely blue

But knowing that we can be cool and knowing you still care
About that fact that I like you and that promising stare
Makes me feel special from the feelings I bare

The dance at the social was one to remember, I even forgot to take a picture
Trapped in a moment in time, so star struck and glamour

The moment was special, and the timing was great
Because the song that was played was the last one, they taped

Vitamin C graduation "Friends Forever" will be
"As we go on", I'll never forget the time you spent with me

Bride and the Groom

I think I'm in love which is something I seek
It's not like it's a bad thing and it's not like he's a geek

He's just stuck on stupid, I mean stuck on Kara
From the person I thought it was before, I'd truly prefer Sarah

I mean ain't nothing wrong with Kara, I'm saying it like some sort of dike
But I know he could've done betta & had anyone in sight

Maybe I'm saying me; maybe I'm not
I'm not judging anyone and I'm not specific; on the spot

Because to me it can't be serious; there are other dudes out there
But the way I feel now; is something like a scare

Because I felt this same way before about a homie and a friend
So maybe this is just a phase and someday soon it'll end

But now as I write; I love him even more
Or maybe it's just a phase; I'm not so sure

But as the rain still falls and the flowers still bloom
I'll care about Jake; like people care about weddings with a bride and the groom

Feelings at Sought

Sometimes I wonder why it all happens to me
Why it snapped at me? Why it wasn't meant to be?

It was real I just know it
My attitude at the time didn't show it
But it was sometime that I'd go for it

Like rain on summer nights
I feel like crying
Like dying from suicide
Mesmerized by something not in my control

But realizing it now
I wonder how it would have worked
If I wasn't being a jerk, but it can't be my fault
It was my feelings at sought

9 October 2004

Old Flame

I know it not seem like it, but I really loved you
I may have caught attitudes, but inside I adored you

You meant the world to me and made me realize
That somewhere out there you can find someone who truly cares & see right in their eyes

The way I see it is; Roses are red, and violets are blue
I want you to know that I'm truly sorry and that I love you

11 October 2004

Continuously

Like the rain on summer nights outdoors
My heart pours, pours, and pours
For your love to be with me
In every thought I see complete
I don't care what people think
Without our love we're incomplete
And now I realize without you my world would die

Now I don't know what I would do if I was alone and didn't have you
You mean the world & everything to me; without your love I'm incomplete
There's nothing in those simple stores that I adore like you, mi amore
What I'm saying I'm not sure
All I know is my heart soars continuously

Somewhere far off

Senseless. Crazy
I feel insane
Love. Marriage.
Somewhere in Maine

Places to share with others as a thought
People to care for & no one at fault

No one is right, no one is wrong
No one overconfidently accurate
Stay Healthy and Strong

Having self-esteem with choices and having faith in my heart
About the goodness and love in every thought

Because someday you'll need it; someday it'll pay off
Maybe it'll start on Monday or somewhere far off

Emptiness

Lonely without that person who truly cares about you
Feeling empty inside like others despise you
Suddenly realizing that being without that person
Having a difficult moment, troubling to move on, needing a diversion
Like empty holes are not being filled in
Like rose petals blooming without the field
Deserted in a maze with no one there to help you
Everyone else found an escape, except you...

18 October 2004; 1:10pm-1:20pm

Missing you

I miss you so much and I've been so horrible to you. I am so sorry please accept my apology. You are the only one I truly care about and if I wanted to move on I couldn't. You're the only person that I've felt involved with and we ain't even smash; so right now, it's hard for me to move on. I know you feel like you didn't make a mistake, but I know I did, and I need you to know that.

P.S. I love you and care so much...

Through the hard times

There will be moments in our relationship
When times will get hard I know
These words are to get you through these times
To help us grow.

I need you to know how much I care
And how true my feelings are for real
I know I my heart that you hold the key
God showed me in time because I felt my heart heal.

From all the hurt and all the pain
The trembles and tears
You found your way to me & never letting go
You showed me how much you cared.

In just a short time, you've given me the grace
That God showed you how to do
God's mercy is everlasting
I know this because I see it in you.

In the way you smile
In the way you laugh and in the way, you treat me so
In the way we kiss, oh how I miss those lips; I never want to let you go.

But on some serious business
The summer will be our fun
Once August gets here and the semester starts
Here's my promise to you that I won't run.

My calls may decrease
My text may be short, and my letters may slowly go away
Just know that I'm focused & that school is almost over
And I'll never be too far away.

I will think of you always; I'll do my best to call on the short that I have
Don't hold the distance to my heart, but to my head it's never intentional for me to be distant, so
bad.

I care about you
You mean the world to me; you shown me so much gentle, loving, kindness, and it shows
This poem is to get you through the hard times
So that you know, yo mean everything to me, next to God, the most.

Spiritual Influences

Sometimes I don't even know what I'll be listening to on TV
Vampires, demons, the fight for love, crime, Immortality
What you watch and what you listen to, becomes an example of who you become
Its sets the role of positive or negative in your mood, that type of mindset and your personality it
transforms
Be careful with who and what you surround yourself with
Speaking negative, or aspirations of positive, becomes the type of atmosphere you're enrolled in
Movies, music, commercials, and books
Friends, enemies, coworkers, spiritual leaders, or play a role in the way we look
At different things, the way we move, also the way we walk
To the expressions we choose to make, the nonverbal, all influence the way we talk
Which is why it's important to continue to surround yourselves with more nurturing things
We need to focus not on material possessions, the approval of others, or any of these worldly
means

Vulnerable hours

I'm home.
I'm comfortable and I'm Vulnerable
In my own space.

I am comfortable and I'm vulnerable

You asked me if I live alone
That makes me uncomfortable and vulnerable

Only because I know I get turned on easily,
Because I'm comfortable in my own home, now I am vulnerable
You say you have self-control
You say you just want us to get to know
Each other as a whole
That's your goal

I can't... I am comfortable and I am too vulnerable

I'd be too tempted to take you on, after I play my favorite song,
You asked me what color panties I have on...
Damn I'm turned on

Yes, I'm getting too comfortable and too vulnerable.

All I have is my panties on
Sometimes the music turns me on,
Sometimes being too close gets me going,
Especially since it's been too long

It makes me comfortable and really vulnerable.

You're sexy and it's on, our bodies bumping to the song,
I'm pretty sure I just felt you're hard on,
You gotta go

Now I'm just vulnerable!!!

2014

I don't want to be the girl that keeps reminding you of your past
Have that same nonchalant attitude, texting you with my stupid ass
Shit, bullshit, never letting the past go, we both did each other wrong, same sex, different show
All has been forgiven, in and out of church we both prayed
How can we move on past the bad behavior, when we still bring up the same things
I am not referring to let's be a new you, a new me
We wouldn't be who we are now, if we didn't learn from the wrong things
But, somehow someway, yesterday is still old
It's lost, the bridge is burnt, the presents now, there's time for a new goals
I'm sure forgive, don't forget, and our minds, we're all human beings
This doesn't mean we have to hurt each other over and over again, it's a new year, a fresh start in
the year 2014

Relapse

Consumer relapse after a crack-consumes kryptonite

Watching that powered material take over that maternally figure
Your first eyes, ears, and sound into this world.

That first breath, that first bite, fetal positioning sonogram site,
Underneath the consistent heartbeat. Conception. The beginning.

Watching the first burst of smoke absorption get inhaled.
The first inhale, first pipe, first flame from such a small object which ignites into the air, against
that first pipe and burnt spoon.

When you see that first pipe, that small object that ignites,
Against that maternal figure, your first sight, as it takes over all the right, slow to speak, no
control. Silence.

The substance has taken over, it controls the vibration of the voice. Can easily be identified in
any activity especially over the phone.

Irritated.
Frustrated.

Frequent relapse.

Paragraph #1

Absence
Another word for escape
Another-phrase do run away
Another way to take breaks
Another way to
Announce fear
Another way to invite pain
Another way to skip sunshine
Another way to invite insanity
The devil likes confusion
The devil likes pain
The devil likes to play, play mental mind games
This poem is to free me
This poem is to [prove] him wrong
Random thought:
Jason wanted me to write a paragraph
So here's paragraph #1.

Wednesday 25 July 2018

Retrogressed

What is Anti Depressed?
Can it truly be addressed?
In a strange way you can actually
Never truly invest
Is it hurt?
Is it pain?
It drives me insane
To the point where I can only
Address its name
Never sure
Never positive
Always feeling
Their derogative
An immunization
Thoughts of assumptions
But I'm content
What it truly has meant
Keep going
On in life
Sometime fearful of strife
But anti depressed
Still can't be addressed
It has a strain in your veins
Something that can't really be changed
Only retrogress

4 February 2009

Sagittarius

Incredibly handsome, Milky Way, Hershey kiss
My severe charm of infatuation,
I must keep this obedient class
But you have my thoughts wandering off
To our first orientation…
Long Island iced tea,
Slow sips, lemonade, a mix of the devils drink
Your smile, a delightful sparkle, of imperfection
I've never seen such a gap that could be so elegant.
Shallow, I am not, because your voice speaks to me
In words that are unspoken and I know
Deep within me. My soul sees something
That's so complete for me
But I can't get the nerve to stop rambling
When you speak to me.
Deafened ears, defeated breath,
This antsy feeling that I get
Takes control of my inner-being
I get appalled at what happens next
Correction, I'm involved, repulsive thoughts
Mumbled voice, I have stalled, in due time,
I will be able to tell apart
The difference, until then,
I'll continue to be curious, physically, and mentally attracted
You stay on my mind like a distraction, one day
I hope we have some brave interaction

Farewell, Sagittarius

25 April 2012

Take me as I am

What do you want from me?
You got me I'm here til the end
You weren't ready for a relationship
So that's what you got I'm your friend
I am confused again because u claim I don't call you
I say that's insane
I call you I text you you don't answer, I complain
I finally get it across sometimes your busy I understand
So I lessen up on communication and you start to demand
Either let me know what you want because it's a little hard to decline
Yes you're going through stuff but I can't read your mind
One minus I'm complaining assuming the worst
When I stop doing that you complain and it's starting to hurt
I want to be your all you know this and understand
Speak up on how you feel or take me as I am

11 February 2009

Pride Aside

My time is lost
And I guess yours is too
You don't care about me
And I don't care about you
I can move on with my life
Because other people don't interfere with my decisions
I'm frustrated, things just don't matter
Takes to long for you to get it
Ugh is how I feel
And yes I can complain
But if what I try to get out doesn't matter
Then I'm done playing this game
Just leave me alone
I will sing my time to heal and weep
This is just the beginning, there's still time I can seek
Whatever has always been your answer and now it's mine
I'm happy with my life and decision; I've pushed pride aside

Hurt

It hurts me to know
It hurts me to go
It hurts to sit here and wait

It's me that you're unsure
It's me that this occurs
Unsure
About me being your soulmate

We're young, we're naïve
We have hopes, we believe
We fail to realize
That love is true

It hurts me to see
It hurts me to be
What I am
And that's in love with you!

Bio Poem

Wanda

Stubborn, goofy, mood-swings and writer Daughter

of William and Debra

Who feels loved by Christ?

Angry when males and females talk shit and

cared for by loved ones

Who needs love, honesty?

And as a helpful stress reliever

Who gives advice?

Unwanted and wanted judgment

and love to those who accept it

who fears pity?

Another broken heart

and creepy crawlers

Who would like to see a wonderful future?

A degree in writing

A California

Resident of Saint Louis City, Mo

Jackson

Better connection

Ever since the accident I've felt closer and closer to you

I realize that life is short and I want to spend as much time as possible with you

But drawing away from me and have become severely controlling and demanding

You've started not to care as much, I need a better understanding

You say you want to be with me and that you love me too

But you're not putting as much effort into it anymore, but I'll continue my love for you

It seems as if you only love me when you want and it doesn't work that way

You love me when I'm distant and when I begin to pull away

I really want to be with you, but you're not giving me the same perspective

You rarely seem, that's your choice, I feel less like a core class and more so an elective

You probably think that poem is a display of everything you're doing wrong

But the truth of the matter is, you haven't fixed these items, these are the same things going on

It's hard to write like this about you, because you're really a great guy

But you're changing, distant, and stating negative comments, it's starting to make me cry

I mean there are a lot of outstanding qualities about you, like your personality, but your feelings aren't affective

This means in order for us to last, I need to feel a better connection

Angel of mine

It's kind of hard being with you when you're away

It seems as if we're never together with you working each day

I mean I'm glad you have a job(s), but sometime s I wish that working was on me

I don't mean to sound conceited, but I care a lot about you, you see

I mean I love you now and I can't stop thinking about you

You're on my mind at home, at school, and my dreams too

So I guess what I'm trying to say is maybe we should talk when you have more time

Cause I still love you and need you

Angel of Mine

Angel in the sky

You never lied to me

You never made me ask why

You never made me do something I was uncomfortable wit h

Maybe that's the reason I cry

You never let me down

You only lifted me up

You were there for me when I needed you

Especially when things became rough

I wonder sometimes why I fell in love with you

I wonder why I couldn't try

Maybe you're more than just that friend to me

You're my angel in the sky

Allow

When I found out I wanted to

be a writer I wasn't surprise d

I was always doing it

So it was always a career in my eyes

I started talking about it in

6th grade At Point School

Ms. Poldan's class the

school was kind of boring

A real pain in the ass

So I guess writings not a

problem Since that ' s

what I'm doing now Even

if it' s also poetry

That's something I'd allow

All that time

Of all the

stress of all the

pain

Of all the things you're going

through I'm the one you sacrificed

I'm the one you patronized

and I was the one hear for

you

It took me to take

action it took me to tell

you

That I was the one who needed space

when we both knew

That you weren't t rue

With your feelings of honestly and grace

You were in denial

you were on trial

You had time to tell me what you felt

inside this whole time you were doubtful

The whole time you were unsure

why did you waste all that time?

Alive or dead

Depressed that's it that's exactly what I feel

Like a tornado in the summer ruining a spring, flowered field

Torn up inside

Torn apart as we know it Paper ripped so

There's no proof to show it

Except I'm that paper

And now I'm scattered into pieces

And folded out of shape

Ensemble creases

So why does the word suicide

Keep popping in my head it's not like anyone cares

If I'm alive or dead

BE A MAN

I'm tired of making you a first

priority when you make an option,

not fine

I'm tired of being that real woman you claim you want

but you can't even put your pride aside

You claim how these women out here ain't real

women

Yet you have one right in front of your eyes

You claim you love me and you want to be with me

Not taking any risks, yeah that's being "on your grind"

Love doesn't wait for your convenience

It doesn't wait for your time

It's shared equally and through communication

Guess I can't really be the one, your feelings you can't even share them with mine

my times it seems runs at a 24hour rate

Like Schnucks, I make it easy

No I'm not perfect, but I try to be for you

Maybe my mistake, like Quick trip, your time fast, quick, "if" and "when" you need

me Barack Obama says, "It's time for a change" I guess that's his new plan

Its 2009, push pride aside

It's time to be a man

A deal with the devil

I'm tired of you cheating you dirty dog

I'm tired of cooking your meals you pathetic hog

All you do is lie all you do is cheat

All I felt while with you was nothing but discrete

All you ever thought about was smashing what you could get

All I ever thought for you was if I even wanted to give you shit

Because the way you treated me was beyond cruel control

And the way I treated you was giving you my heart and soul

So me going back with you aren't on level

Ca use being miserable all over again for you is like making

A deal with the devil

Who am I: A person who cares?

I'm artistic

I'm

creative

I' m intelligent

I'm fun

I love?

I watch movies

Enjoy pictures

I get work

done I'm a

writer

I'm a girlfriend

I'm a reader

I have prayers

I'm an achiever, I'm a

dreamer I'm a person who

cares

Dear Death,

Why haven't we met yet a why are we waiting. It's as if we're trying to work it out and still

debating. What are you waiting for I've suffered enough. I can't stand being alone and with someone it's

still rough. Have you not heard of freak accidents nor do you like my misery? Are you waiting to I'm

pregnant and have complications during delivery. And leave my baby to suffer without his/her mom to

care. And start their misery a new beginning and leave them alone and unprepared.

Love,

Death

Dear Suicide,

Should I do what you say and destroy my life. Should I leave this world never getting a chance to be a wife? Should I just not believe in future love and continue on in after life. Is it that necessary to go to hell and still be stabbed with a knife? Why did you say when there's nothing to live for. You're just going to end up getting hurt and left with an open sore. So do you have a plan for me I ask in concern of honest truth to be told? Are should I continue to live with Pain and hurt as if its silver and gold.

Love,

Suicide

Dear Partial Love,

Why have you giving me it and left it at that. Not having a real ending or new beginning on the

mat. You let me love him and give him my heart. Not having it peaceful at the end now we're farther apart.

Why is it I love him and have sudden dreams? Is or are they coming true is that what you mean. You've left

me confused and tears to cry. Is that why we ended and you left my heart to die.

Sincerely,

Partial Love

P.S. Give me an answer soon

Dear Pain and Suffering,

I'm sick of life and what it has is just shame. For every tragic accident there's someone you blame.

As if it isn't bad enough you have suffered a lost. And you pay off in debts and there's still an

Insincere cost. The hatred in the hearts of those who don't believe. And when a death is sudden a babies

conceived. You bring hurt to me and leave my heart shattered. For every time the phone rings my blood just

clatters. Bringing insincere to all the ones that I love. And joy in the unpleasing hearts of above. I can't go on

with life and how it's a prison cell. Never understanding the concepts and how I failed.

Love,

Pain and Suffering

P.S. Plea se stay away you've caused enough pain

Dear Love,

Do you have a plan for me is that why I live? Is there someone special out there who needs my love to *give?* Is that why I started with partial love and now it's whole. For someone will come along to treat me less like silver and more like gold. Will they love and more like gold. Will they love and care for me as if I were there heart. Will they feel *even* closer to me when we're farther apart? Will they debate whether or not to leave me while there in tears? Tears of joy I mean and take away an all the fears. Will they wait or pause; for the right time to tell me. Or will they com e right out with it so they make e sure not to fail me.

Love,

Love

Dear Hell,

I've visited you already know I'm back again. Are you happy did I leave you with a grin? Do you have that smirk on your face as so when I toured. Did you enjoy stabbing me deeply with your dagger and sword? Were you disappointed in me when I yelled in your face? Or were you expecting it as if you cheated me with disgrace. You couldn't be confused because that's my job. You can't shed tears because I've been there I've sobbed. So do you want another visit or are you going to leave me with peace. Are will you visit me with (Dear death) and give me my deceased.

Your nightmare,

Hell

Different Direction

I know you probably care less

on what I have to say

But give me a change

Cause it's been bothering me everyday

Now I have decided

That I've made the mistake of being horrible to you

I'm so sorry and that's usually hard for me to say

I mean you actually meant a lot to me

and I know I'm young and a lii naive

But now I realize what's important

And I stick with what I believe

So take that into consideration and not as something

from a weak freshman

And hopefully maybe we can be friendlier when greeting

and start in a different direction

Even for me

I have officially given up on boys as of now (8:46p.m Dec. 2 04')

Because most are funny acting towards me and I don't get how

I see myself as pretty most of the time, but not anymore

Because I've been turned down more times than a mob exiting the door

and I wonder at times is it my personality to blame

Because I've turned down so many guys with good personalities it's a shame

I've turned them down sometimes because se of their looks

Instead of who they are on the inside like judging the cover of books

They say you can't judge a book by the cover and now that' s what I see

So what goes around comes around always and that goes even for me

Falling for you

I don't understand what it is about you that bring a smile to my face

I'm confused on why I can't help but laugh to the touch of your warm embrace

When you get close, I can't help but want to scream

It seems as if this is only but a dream

If so I don't want to wake because I'm into you so much

When we're together I can't help but want your sweet touch

I'm falling in love with you from every second and hour of the day

When you don't call me I feel as if you're pulling away

But I tell myself that life is busy and you have a lot to do

And that's where you make up for missed time and call me your boo

You tell me I'm your baby and that I'm your girl

That I'll always be the only one and that I'm your world

You stay true to me and tell me everything so I don't doubt you not even 4 a second or two

And except 4 many more reasons that's why I'm falling for you

Fed up with that stuff

What is it with people and this he said, she said stuff.

It's working my nerves because these people have a habit of thinking their tough

They think it's cute to get caught up in this type of junk

Also, thinking it's cute to bother those quiet types; assuming their punks

Well, it isn't cute to me considering that those types of people get enough

Of taking that shit from you and get fed up with that stuff

Form of weather

Why people are treated different just because of their race

Why do people feel the need to argue in a time where you should embrace?

Why are people excluded just because they're not known by a certain group or clique?

Why do people base their lives on stories, music, or some chick flick?

Why do people make a big deal of little things and give up when they don't understand

Why would a woman give herself up just to prove that she can get a man?

Why does he say, she say seem to get the majority vote of peers

Why is it people want to give up the first site of defeat and break down in tears

Why can't we just get along; when we should all stick together

When families and friends gather for reunions in any form of weather

Happy Birthday, Ilisha

Happy October 29th and a happy birthday it is

You're the greatest friend in the world so make a special wish

What'd you wish for to be in Michael's heart forever?

For love to be always and you to be together

You've been my best friend ever since first grade

You, Brandi, and Harvey are the bested friends I ever made

You've been there for me through those rough times

Even when we didn't get along and I felt like committing a crime

When things were rough you took the time to stand by me and call

So today on this special day I hope you have the greatest birthday of all

Having loved someone so much

Have you ever loved someone so much?

That it hurt inside feeling deprived

When they're doing and saying the same things

To you with someone else

When a slow song comes on you want to break down

When you hear your friends talk about their relationships

You just want to cry inside with no sound

Thinking back only on the good points

But acting out the bad ones

Thinking how it may have been forever,

But something you felt went wrong

Well that's how I feel and I don't think it'll ever go away

Jesus is my Lord and Savior

I was told once by a man, I thought I loved
that I wasn't' being true to myself
And he was exactly right
I was being loyal to my flesh

I'd made a commitment to be foul
I'd made the decision to offend
I became a lust, adulterer, and fornicator
I had been righteous to sin

BUT GOD, transformed me to a new being
No longer was I righteous to sin
Yeah, I backslid, I had my down-falls
But I repented and he picked me up again

When we backslid, God doesn't leave us
we leave him to please ourselves
We make decisions to please the world
but we can't serve two masters
You either serve the Lord, or choose hell

No, I will not apologize for being blunt
All will be judged by the lawmaker, and not
each other,
We have the free will to choose to live right
We have the free will to choose to live
wrong.
But God is and always will be the overall
Eternal - decision maker.

When you make a decision to turn
your life around
This isn't a decision that has to please man
When God creates you to be made new
Just remember it was his only son, Jesus,
Who died for YOUR SINS?

No one is holier than thou; Let him who is
without sin cast the first stone
The truth is not in us, if we say we have no
sin, we deceive ourselves.
The gift of God *is* eternal life through Jesus Christ
our Lord, but for the wages of sin is death.

I'm done quoting the bible for now
I just wanted to make it fairly clear
I made the decision to get my house in order
because the end is very near

I made the final decision to follow Jesus
I made the final decision to live according to
his word and to lead not on my own
understanding, to endured forever

I made the final decision to fight my battles
the right way, in my war room
To gain a closer more intimate relationship
with Jesus, My Lord and Savior.

23 September 2015

Time to get right

We pray for a healing
To be healed from the devils disease,
But do us the time to truly talk to GOD And
understand what the power of prayer really
means.

Prayer is a sacred time to talk to our Savior Prayer
is a treasured time to understand what level of
GOD really ranks,
Prayer is not only a time to complain and ask for
what we don't have
Prayer is a time to give God and his son his honor
and worthy thanks.

Thank him for the breath of life
Thank him for the gift of peace,
Thank him for his natural light
Thank him for this time to think.

Think about how he saves your soul each day
by waking you up and enjoying another day to
grow individually,
Just because you go to church and shout Hallelujah
Doesn't mean you're saved, it doesn't make you
Holy.
Repenting is a marvelous thing
It means you have another chance to change,
It means you have another chance to shout "God
you're Merciful"
I don't deserve the blessings you continue to
Maintain.

We should be rejoicing in his Everlasting Love
we should be rejoicing in his unconditional love
for our hearts,
We should take the time out to say thank you
because it's so easy to die before tomorrow.

When your light switch turns on
Shout "Hallelujah"
When your car starts shout "amen,"

Give thanks to Jesus
Because he delivered your soul from sin.

Even if you ride the bus to school
or have to walk each and every day,
Give thanks to the everlasting God above
because he's the one who paved the way.

You didn't do this by yourself
Just because you go to work and grind
Your job isn't a guaranteed spot
God was holding it for you every time.

I'm not the perfect person
But I'm perfect in his image,
He started me on my way, each and every day
so he's worthy to be remembered.

Remembered for all the times I blew my money on
stupid things,
And how I still have a roof to lay my head
Remembered for all the times I cursed people out
with the same tongue I ask him to provide for
safety in the place I lay my head to rest

He forgives me even when I lose my temper and
complain when things aren't going my way, And
even when I don't speak righteousness
He forgives me anyway.

This isn't an excuse to continue to sin
Just because he loves us and his mercy doesn't fail,
there will come a time, if we don't get right with
Jesus now
Nothing will be able to save our souls from the
fiery pits of hell.

26 May 2014

True Wealth

The most important lesson I've learned in my life is that " the greater part of our happiness or misery depends on our d is position, and not our circumstances"-Maliha Washington

It's been many time s I've woken up in the morning, contemplating on how I should live my life. I have the se constant de bated with myself about how to be the perfect girlfriend, the perfect friend, the perfect sister, the perfect daughter, the perfect child of God, the perfect employee, and more. Then, I come to the conclusion that perfect doesn't exist. I can only live my life according to me , accept the fact that no matter how nice I am to others or ho w many things 've success fully done in my community, at the end of the day , 1 have to be satisfied with me. It doesn't take having all the money in the world to be happy nor having the latest fashion. If I actually sit down, re la x, and begin to look at all the great things God has done for me, this is true wealth. One quote that I've come across is "If one measures all the things they do not have, they'll never have enough. If one measure s all the things they do, they'll have more than enough." It's all too often I try to find ways to make myself happy, when happiness starts at home. Until I can be happy with myself there's no one person or one item that will be able to make me happy until, I'm happy with me. I've ma de many excuses from time to time on why I am not happy with the way my life is going. No one has the answer to everything. I will say that the journey begins with living life and not thinking about how to live it.

8 October 2011; 8:59pm

Intimacy

Sexual frustrations
Lustful altercations
deliberately questioning
Whether to self-fulfill penetration

Google search for Ebony porn
2 fingers spread apart, vibrations on watching
these lost souls, interact in activity, for
money videos sold, separately
Clear
history
Resentful

Disbelief
How could I scoop so low, literally,
unforgiving to someone so close
and expect God to forgive me

The deepest secrets, to the
grave, the truth we all have to
face
What's done in the dark comes to light
on Judgment day we will face

Until then, I will let it all go
Understandingly, I know
I want to be better
Gods will endured forever
the lamb's book of God
My name will be printed,
signed, sealed, delivered

From this moment I will have faith,
through the grace of God, I will wait,
firmly trusting and believing
That I am so much more than intimacy

We Use to be in Love

We use to be in love
The grove, Hallway intellect
yours mile, my mind
Promiscuous, nevertheless

Kindhearted, monogamy
Sensual ... I your queen
self-expression, no secrets
High school sweethearts,
Cherry burst (yea) I mean "it"

The struggle, back & forth, BS
making up, making love
Couldn't break our bond
Romeo/Juliet

We use to be in love
off to college we went
I slipped up, she slipped in
I went through with keyshia Cole's I should have cheated

We use to be in love
our bond, you forgave,
one of the 7 deadly sins
one night I found out,
Unlocked phone, Damn it's a Him!!

Tears I cried,
All the lies between us both, took years to build up trust,
yet seconds to knock it down...
Loyalty, what a joke

We once were in love
At one point, being alone was unseen
Separation, distance traveled
The occasional sexual Fling

I used to be in love
you use to be too
With each other, that was the ideal picture
I could never imagine the day I couldn't be with you, an unwanted vision

I knew it, our family knew it,
It was in the stars up above
Life threw us for a loop
We use to be in love!

Christ Like

I serve a wonderful God
a merciful God
My savior, Jesus Christ, he loves me so
Through his will I can conquer all,
 through his will I want to go

Through the storm, through the rain,
I know I'm protected through it all
because I know my God loves me,
Through my praise, through my worship,
on the main line I will call

I'm unworthy of his love
I know I'm not living right
Premarital sex, unforgiving heart, the devils drink,
 I struggle with this ungodly fight

I have to give up these worldly things,
 To gain Christ's unconditional love &
peace I desire to be more like Christ
I have to put down this drink

It controls me, it takes over me
Lusts endeavors ruin my goals
There comes a time where you have to decide
is hell deserving of your soul

2014 is here,
It's a day after new years
Repent and forgive
It's not for others approval to decide,
for our sins he did die
What kind of life will you live???

Thank you Lord

I thank you Lord for my electricity

I thank you u Lord for my car

I thank you Lord for my food, she later, water r, and clothing

I thank you u Lord for my beating heart.

I thank you Lord for my job

I thank you Lord for my peace

I thank you Lord for the things I take for granted

I thank you Lord for providing my every need.

I thank you Lord for my friends and family I

thank you Lord even for my enemies

It's because of these worldly things, that you died for us Lord

So I thank you Lord for cleansing me

Cleansing me Lord from a world of sin

I thank you Lord for my dog and my loving boyfriend

I thank you Lord for technology and education

So that I may share my praise and worship for you Lord with friends

my thanks is for you Lord and your word for me

My thanks for you Lord will continue on

I thank you Lord for my gift of writing and ministry to

use it to praise your name Lord, forever more

26 May 2014

Concentrate on Me

I am not the same girl.
I accept the truth
Instead of talking about my goals I am living
them, proof
I am living them truth I am
living them free
I begin to watch my own life transform Instead of
watching TV
Instead of watching you pleased Instead of
watching you tease
I no longer watch BS I
review it & leave
I'm no longer focused on him simply
anticipating relief
Cause if I continue to worry about how you feel I can't actively
concentrate on me.
(And vice versa)
#micropoem
#suddenlyinspired
#naturalwriter
#naturalpoet
#poetrylife
#free
#thinking clearly
#Healing

5 March 2017

Marry me today

Do you feel like you can tell me everything?

Do you feel as if anywhere could describe the place for you to sing?

Are you embarrassed by me in public or do you enjoy showing me off

Does holding me make you feel too sensitive and romantic or does it make you feel soft

If you could do anything for me to make me happy what would it be?

Would you do anything and everything to fulfill my needs?

Does being with me show that there is hope and love out there for all

Would you be there to pick me up when I fall?

Can you not get me off your mind and miss me when I'm away

And if we were old enough do you think you'd marry me today

Lips are sealed

Overall, what I'm trying to say is

That you're really stressing me out and I love you a lot

you accuse me of getting an attitude to quickly

Yet you're the one stirring the pot

You probably believe that I'm a pest

And that I think there's nothing good about you

but the truth is, yes I am a pest

I am because I care for you

Tyrone this is a plea from me

Baby I'm trying to keep this as real as I can

Sometimes I believe that you don't care anymore about me

Just the ideas; that's all you understand

I'm not putting you down

Just rising you up and letting you know how I feel

but this is the last time I hope

So for now my lips are se ale d

My Chocolate Thunder

The stress in my life has

caused me a lot of pain

Worrying about things that don't matter

has driven me insane

When things in my life go good

I can't help but wonder

what it would be like

Without Ty

My chocolate thunder

My Ultimate Goal

It's amazing to me what people would do today

How they'd do anything; rat out anybody just to get their way

Stabbing their friends in the back just for attention

They make the first punch when fighting then complain about suspension

People of the same race; who'd think they'd get along

They have disagreements like lyrics in a controversial rap song

What they talk about is the truth yet those haters put them down

And when things catch up with them they want to leave town

Not understanding why people do these things can be stressing to the soul

Because making a difference just for one simple thing would be my ultimate goal

My Own Dreams

How is it I love someone and not want to be friends?

How is it I can share everything but when it's all over just put it to an end?

How is it I feel like giving up on some of the most important moments of my life?

Just because things don't work out perfectly and other obstacles give me strife

How it is that love can hurt but it's supposed to be the key to my heart

How is it I can feel close to someone yet I can feel farther apart

How it is love can make me do some of the craziest things

How is it I have goals but don't believe in my own dreams?

Petrifying Chatter

Loving you is like loving myself

I'm obsessed and I love you to death

I don't give a care about what anyone ways or do

I'm in love with you cause you're my boo

You're very important to me and have a wonderful personality

so I plan to stay with you; I can't believe this is reality

I like your sneeze, your demeanor, and style

So hopefully your love for me is also on file

I know I'm true to you with my heart and soul

and you're committed to me like fire does coal

We wonderful for each other and that's all that matters

so the hell with those whispers and petrifying chatters

Endeavor

Guidelines

Sidelines

Truth

Second geometry

Advanced business

Creative error

Amor es Azul y casa

English

Lies

Endeavor

Bright and Shining Star

"Hey" I said hesitating not knowing whether to speak

because the thought of you leaving my hearts incomplete

'Tm sorry" I said anyways as you said what's p

When you said that were you being polite, serious, or what

You said it as if you missed me and hated me in a way

so I understand how you feel right till this day

The moment we stared at each other in that complete silence

what a moment reasonable without arguing or violence

A moment of terror struck through my heart and passed

Thinking you weren't going to say anything and take of really fast

but you didn't and it shows how mature you really are

I loved you for that my Bright shining star

Brings me death

Have you ever been heartbroken, guess not since you seem so confident?

Have you been depressed not knowing when you're going to get your next compliment?

Have you not felt pain of so many deaths closing around you?

Feelings as if you can't continue life and decide it's over it's through

you haven't felt solitaire since everyone seems to know you

But it's not the same for me cause unlike you I don't have friends who stay true

you see life as nothing, but a joke

I see life as cancer; you're going to die eventually if you take more than one smoke

well for me I continue going on as it is anyways

Since it seems for me to have more good and less bad days

It seems to continue great without you because I stay true to myself

and I'm going to continue being me until life brings me death

I love you

You're my mother

And you're my girl

You're my best friend

And you're my world

You take great care of me

with all your heart even

when I bug you

Like annoying wheels on a cart

We chill and hang out

like friends do in clubs

We understand each other

Unlike Jerry Springer slugs

But that doesn't matter much

what matters is you

I hope you get well and

remember I love you to

e

es a damn about me No one freaking cares

nd broke it off with me and at school there's mean mugging stares

ample, I thought I had friends but now to them I don't exist

absent from school I'm not even missed

about me like they know me but only know my name

me not even that but when I catch an attitude they go insane

gives a damn?

ust collides

what the answer to that is it's easy

e

I've already died

I haven't felt this much pain since the day of your accident

I haven't felt this much pain since my god father and granddaddy died

I haven't felt this much pain since December 8, 2007

When I told you I needed space and you hung up, not long after I cried

I cried the whole day, I cried the whole afternoon,

I cried the whole night until I fell asleep I

suffered nightmares, I suffered deeply I

called you, you hung up on me

I feel like crying now

Even though I don't know why I put myself through all of this

you're unsure about us; you're stressed out about life

Is this the reason I couldn't get a kiss

There was nothing I could do to make this better

There was not thing I could say, but I still tried

I still attempt this friendship with you

But somehow I feel as if I've already died

Kindness in your soul

Why is the world so angry with violence and discrete?

Why do families split up and leave loved ones unrelieved

Why does everyone disrespect each other as if no one means anything in their heart?

What's the point of lying when you're bound to get caught?

What's the point of cheating when you're eventually bound to feel shame?

It's called a conscience so there's no one you can blame

What's the point to marrying if you're just going to divorce?

What's the point of working it out if you're going to make the other choice?

What's the point of being happy when someone's bound to make you mad?

What's the point of anti-depressants when that makes you even sadder?

Why is there anger management when you should have self-control?

What's the point of hatred when there should be kindness in your soul?

Insincere price

Dreams are things

That only you can make come true.

Believing in them is easy to say,

But harder to do

Life brings confusion and pain

That's why we have

Goals in life

And making a mistake

Without setting things straight

Can result in an

Insincere price

In the World

Get out of my face cause you wasting my time

You better get your attitude checked before I become a suspect in your untimely homicide crime

You think people (especially females) want you, but they really don't

It's only the money you have and material things you but they really want

You get on our nerves and act as if you are a fag

It's not cute neither sexy either when you let your pants sag

Instead of looking thuggish and calling yourself a pimp

When it all comes down to help a friend you back down like a wimp

So get out of my face and quit calling me your girl

Because I really wouldn't care if you were the last male in the world

In the first place

Never give someone all your love because they'll use it to get back at

you Once they find someone else they'll tell you your relationships

through They'll stab you in the front and leave you heart broken

Then you express your true love for them

and they're on the first train smoking

they don't care about how you feel once

you gave them what they want

Now your left depressed and memories or regret come back to haunt

your left devastated and hurting inside

And once it really gets to you your heart collides

you start missing them a whole lot

When you're lonely and sad

Then anger hits you and you steam up really bad

Start wondering why you were ever interested in such horrible taste

then wonder why you wanted to get involved with them

In the first place

Who am I: Human Being?

Who am I?

I'm a person with life

a soon to be mother

a son to be wife

I'm an achiever, I'm a dreamer

I'm a worrier that cares

I'm a believer, I have religion

on I'm a person with prayers

I've suffered lost; I've gained priority

I' m a soon to be college student

Leader of sorority

I'm a student with attitude

who enjoys sing?

Just like you I have goals in life

I'm a human being

Life

Why do people judge others off the way they look?

Why do people always say things that hurt others like every name in the book?

Maybe it's because they don't care about others feelings

Maybe it's because people are rude and have no sense of feelings

Why do people take violence as a first result?

Why is it people can't take criticism as truthful advice instead of an insult

What is it about people wanting to give others all kind hell and strife?

Instead of minding their business, so those who care can live their own life

To be your wife

When I think of you heart collides

Cause I miss you dearly and it hurts inside

It hurts that you don't want to see me and don't even speak anyone

Cause of how I treated you when we were together before

I wish it was different and we should have been friends

So you wouldn't have hatred towards me and we didn't have end

I cry for you sometimes because you were so real to me

And now I ruined us because it was hard to deal with me

I feel tortured and ashamed because I' m lonely without you

When you were so sweet to me I was crazy about you boo

But now it's over and I can't move on

The memories replay in my head like a dreadful song

I tried to get over you, but it's impossible you see

And now you can't even stand to even **look** at me

The way you looked before was so positive and cool

And the way I treated you was way beyond cruel

I thought you were playing me at first but now I know

Body Freeze

Deeper and deeper big daddy

is where I prefer you to go?

Faster and faster until my flesh can't take any more

yet, then still I don't want to stop just slowly it down a bit

Nice and slow, back and forth

don't stop baby please don't quit

Push harder and harder I love it when it's rough

now slow once again babe I can't get enough

Your kisses your touch on my neck somehow makes me weak in my knees

the coldest of your tongue me tingle and my body freeze

Cherish friendship forever

I am in love with my best friend

The one who's stuck with me through thick and thin

We've known each other for all these years

We've cried, we've fought, and shared thoughts for future careers

I love him for what he believes and out friendship we've always conceived

I've always thought what doesn't kill you makes you stronger

And my love for him not coming back only makes me think longer

Why can't I have him as more than the best?

For he's one of the few food men unlike all the rest

He's filled with special, goodness and hope in his heart

Now I can't stand the thought of moving and being apart

For he's the key that treasures my soul

Without it I'd as empty y as coal empty; empty inside with no hope

Unclean, unfresh, like a bath without soap

Except he's that glue that holds me together

And I'll always cherish our friendship forever

Working my nerves

My most fear for afterlife is going to hell

But that probably wouldn't matter because my future as of now is probably juvenile or jail I

mean my daddy is working my nerves; I'm feeling displeasure and pain

If I don't get away now I think I might go insane

Now I see what my oldest brother went through and why he wanted to move on Cause

this shit is getting old like a played out ass record and song

But its life and going on in here isn't normal; more like a nightmare than dream But I

try to forgive and forget for the lord and savior upstairs

Because I want to live life to the fullest and go heaven prepared I

know all life I won't go through this much longer

And plus what doesn't kill me is making me stronger

So forget this, move on because life isn't a straight path, but has cracks and different curves but in

the back of my mind this shit is always working my nerves

Work of art

Dying for you is so easy for me

Because I'm deeply in love with you is that hard for you to see I'd

commit murder for you if you need me too

The thought of suicide if our whole relationship was through I'd be

there for you in a time of need

I'd give you my heart if you needed it to breathe

you're my world and mature in your heart

To me you're a masterpiece and a wonderful work of art

Wish

I wish there was no violence

I wish there was no crime

I wish people didn't have to die

I wish there was still time

I wish I wasn't so stressed

I wish broken didn't explain my heart

I wish my dad and I were

Closer together instead of farther apart

I wish that life was fair

So no one would get turned down

I wish things could be a l it t le different in turning my life around

Something's would be great to take back

Because they're plenty of regrets

I wish life could be a little perfect instead of stress, pain, and life threats

Willing to lose

I continue to push; because I love you

I continue to help you through; because I care

I tell you: you can; because I believe in you

And through all ups and downs; like us; we've been there

I continue to try hard because you're my inspiration

I continue to believe because we're meant to be

I tell you I love you because it's true

And when we're upset with each other like anorexia I can't eat

I can't stand it when we're mad towards each other

I can't stand it when my attitude gets the best of me too

so I will try to continue to work more on it

Because that's one thing; you; I'm not willing to lose

Whose fighting who

The teenagers of today are working my nerves so much it makes me want to spit

The majority act so funny to friends; fake and so full of shit

They do anything to fit in and to get attention

They argue a fight then complain about suspension

They don't care about school or passing; they only come to school for the drama

He said, she said it's giving my brain trauma

How are you able to focus on peers all day and still concentrate on work?

Main focuses on fighting and continues to act like a jerk

it doesn't seem to connect with me maybe it does to you

Because my work overall is most important not whose fighting who

Who belongs together?

Your every word in my ear s are so encouraging, so pleasuring, so sensual

Your hands and arms around me make me feel; loved, safe, alive, and invincible

I'm loving yo steeze, yo style, yo demeanor

I'm the jealous type so flirting can cause me to commit a minor misdemeanor

What I love about you is yo sense of style

I don't understand what exactly it is about you that drive me wild

I believe that I'd want to be with you no matter the time, day, or weather

I enjoy yo company and seriously believe it's us who belongs together

When you fall

When I look at myself in the mirror what do I see

I see this beautiful brown female wondering why no one cares for me

Cares enough to want to listen, cares enough to be rea l

Cares enough to stop running and find somewhere to be still

See you don't back out on a friend when they need you the most

When things get tough you don't act as if you've seen a ghost

You stare it in the face and talk to it too

Find out the reason why it's there and is there some way to get through

you trusting a friend and don't doubt t hem when their wrong

You stay true to yourself be less weak and mostly strong

You have a close relationship and don't fail to keep secrets

Not find the nearest associate and tell them and not keep it

You don't go behind their back and talk about their life

As if you didn't know them then give them all kind of strife

When they confront you don't lie, when they have established you know

you don't try to steal their boyfriend and treat them like a hoe

That's not a friend and you should know that ya'll

a friend is honest, cool, and there when you fall

When I say I love you

Tyrone when I say I love you it means I care in my heart

It means I can't help, but miss you when we're farther away apart

it means I'm willing to trust you when trust involves love

It means communicating well within me as I do when I think about the stars above

it means I care enough to listen to your plea when you're feeling down and blue

It means even if I can't stand you sometimes my feelings for you are still true

It means that I can still love you when I'm down and you still love me when things are up

it means even through our arguments and when things are corrupt

We will still be there for each other when our times and needs are due

But most of all my love will be there and that's what it means, Tyrone

when I say I love you

What you didn't do all along

I hate you boy you can kiss my ass

We are officially over so you're a blur in my pass

Being sprung over you was like being sprung over

lice you're so damn irritating; weren't all that polite

You needed anger management; you needed to cool

down Every time someone pissed you off; your temper

left town

I was tired of your attitude; I was tired of your days

I didn't really like you, so now what do you have to say

Except that we're through and I've moved on

now someone can do what you didn't do all

along

No longer feeling me

I know that you're stressed
I know you have a lot going on
I know I'm a pain sometimes
What else am I doing wrong?
Lately it's been hard to have a conversation with you
Without you insisting that I'm pissing you off
But you think that I'm blaming you of being an awful guy
Yet, I'm the one being put off
You don't want to see me
But you say you don't have anytime
In order for us to be together
It's your responsibility to make time
I try to talk to you about your problems
Yet, you don't want to talk and tell me to leave it alone
It's my job as your girl and a friend to be concerned about you
But you make me feel like I'm in the wrong
I really find it hard to understand you
And I wish that you could just see
That I'm hurting because there's this awful thought inside
That you are no longer feeling me

Ain't Nobody Equipped

Strawberries n shortcake
Peaches n cream
Some people can't get it through their head
That I don't care what they mean
I don't have hatred towards people
Believe me that ain't the case
But the people I get stuck with
A put you out for a chase
They talk about how this person did this
And this person did that
Then turn around and be all up their face
Like some absorbed cat
They say ohh they hella fake
Or I can't stand them
Then you agree
Next, their demanding
The explanation from you
About how "you" were the one who said this
Then you tell so and so what was said
Now they're ready to throw fist
I didn't say that
She just saying that to cover up
Knowing that the stories vice versa
Now the person wants to know what's up
They ask you
"Are you mad at me?" I just said that....
(You reply) What?
You left me hanging back there, now that fucked up
Well anybody with he say she say
Going to get slapped in the lips
Because that's too much drama and
Ain't nobody equipped

All my need

I apologize for my rudeness towards you
Apologize for my cruelty involving you
I apologize for not telling you how I feel
Not letting you know if my love for you was real
I feel like apologizing
For making stupid mistakes
But learning from my choices
Is all that it takes
I loved you for you
And love me for me
My love remained mostly
For you like honey and a bee
Rose petals on a flavor
Gardens in a spring
The warmness of teddy bears
And the slow songs that you sing
Like music in the air
And slow songs on the radio
Like juicy fruit gum
And the rings in spaghetti-os
Except I don't need a ring
You're enough for me
Hearing your voice in the telephone
Was all I need

Funeral broke

When I commit suicide
Should I jump off a cliff?
Or maybe a building
Forget it you get my drift
Stab myself in the stomach
Because the back is already taken
From the fakeness of friends
So now my brain is just shaken
Unprescribed meds or
Electrocution is alright
Except for the pain so maybe a drive-by
With my luck will happen tonight
I should cut my vain
It would happen much swifter
Or maybe get pregnant
So my dad a do the job quicker
Nah, that won't work
Since no one likes me that much
So I'll run from the police
Get shot down or handcuffed
And try to fight it
Kicking and screaming
Then they'll have to shoot me
For tonsil misdemeanant
LEDELLEEEEEEEEE
But right now depression a due
Since stress has passed
And that time is renewed
But who cares anyhow
This poems probably some sort of joke
But when it's that time
They'll be sorry and funeral broke

Empty and Scampered

I felt so alone
I felt so deprived
I felt like a stuffed animal
Except without the feeling inside
I felt like I'd been played like some dirty trick
Like I had real friends
Who flicked on and off?
Like a light switch
What am I doing?
In this world I mean
I don't even have a meaning
And I don't have a screen
Unlike some people
With real big families and fancy houses
I live in an apartment
With fighting violent spouses
But I guess everybody has problems
And always will have issues
So why do feel like I'm crying
With someone else's dirty tissues
But I guess that's just a question
That will have not been answered
Stuck there in the back of my mind
Empty and scampered

How I once was

Inside my heart I know that I love him
He's everything I've ever wanted, and I put no other dudes above him
Yet, I hurt inside always because of one of the things he does
But I try to get over it and remember how my life once was
I use to be alone, bored, lifeless, and depressing
But it seems now that I've lost my innocence to him, my life's more stressing
I feel I've given him everything to him, yet I don't think it's enough
When I start feeling deeply admirable towards him things seem to get rough
I tell him how I feel yet sometimes I don't think he understands
Sometimes I feel as if maybe it's much harder in a relationship for him being the man
Is it that I don't understand that he's actually trying hard to please me
That thing is actually stressful for him since my biggest fear of him is to leave me
Yet every time I turn around I feel like he's bringing me down
Leaving me with his family I ain't use to yet every time I look around
I've never been this upset before; it's the second day I've cried two days in a row
Maybe things are going to fast maybe they're going to slow
I just figured the day I gave myself to him and the moment I said I love you was enough trust in me he needed
Or maybe, it isn't him that's the problem maybe it's me
Yet, it seems every time I get mad at him it's for the same reason all the time
But to him I'm the problem it's my fault it's my crime
I love my baby a lot maybe it's something I haven't done yet
So maybe when I get mad a lot, he thinks of what's missing and gets upset
Sometimes I don't think he's trying hard enough because remember I'm only mad at that one flaw he
does
So maybe he doesn't know what he's doing wrong and I'm stressing him about how I once was

Letting go

You lay me down; my legs open wide
My insides are shaky; the outside shows pride
I'm excited yet I'm scared what did I get myself into
He move towards me and adds flavor, it's not too late; I think I'm through
I can't go through with this, but the pina colada starts rushing down my clit
I'm all wet; pretty sure I'm sticky yep; this is the moment this is it
He moves in for the start; he's looking at me' please don't
I'm embarrassed sort of scared, I won't go through with this I won't
I put the pillow up farther over my face; I laugh a little bit
He pulls the pillow back down; he wants to see me; I can't believe he's going through with this
He's a little unsure about it I can tell by the look in his eye
I try to relax and I giggle so I guess I'll give it a try
He finally moves in and I feel his wet tongue try it out
I'm thinking oh my gosh my freaking clit touched the tongue in his mouth
He doesn't like it I'm sure so I might as well get up now
So I move myself out of his way, but he stops me (wow)
He asks me what I'm doing and tells me to lie back down
I'm unsure but I still do it because this makes me curious now
I give him a funny look and he goes back down between my legs
He gets closer and closer to my legs; he moves them more; now their truly spread
He starts to do it again this time a little faster; then slow
I'm feeling out of this world I start to moan; my face I'm sure now is a glow
He's moving his tongue deeper I think he's getting use to it
I start moving my legs around his head; he's reached my clit
This feeling is unbearable it's becoming irrisistably good and amazing
At this point I'm officially turned on; I've began to start shaking
This is what happens when we originally have sex
This is the time where I can't help but to wonder what comes next
This is the time where basically I'd give in to anything because I'm weak
I'm feeling incredibly tired and lazy after this I'm going to sleep
But he's not letting up he begins to stop; I raise up and I notice he's excited
He unzips his pants then unbuttons them to my vagina his self he's invited
But I don't care I've become entirely vulnerable and weak
I'm even more wet; I've came, it's easy to slip in and finally reached his peak
He slips in with no problem and he started pushing deeper inside
I start moaning much closer together
I'm happy, but tired
My boo is a true love maker he knows the spot and where to hit it
He makes me feel like I'm the only girl that he's gave it to and meant it

You're not listening

You're not ready to handle this conversation
So you're not listening
You're watching TV
So you're not listening
So you're tired
You're not listening
I'm just a nagging girlfriend
So you're not listening
You're a guy
You're not listening
I tell you how I feel
You're still not listening
I tell you that
You're not listening
I prove I'm right
You weren't listening
You get pissed off; you take it out on me
All because
You didn't listen
Silence...
I tell you I need to think
I tell you I need time
I'll call you back later
I'll talk to you another time
Thang up
My eyes water
I go to the restroom
I've called you back
(Once again) I've thought of your feelings
I ask you a question
I brought up what just happened
(Once again) you've put it passed you
I guess you're still "not listening"

I'll Miss

I'm sorry that I stress you out
I'm sorry that I bug you a lot
I'm just trying to be a good girlfriend to you
But if that's not what you want I'll stop
You tell me you don't want to talk about your problems
You tell me to leave it alone
Yet, when I'm in the same situation, I have to let it ould
To me that sounds contradicting & wrong
I don't think you're a bad guy
And I'm still into you a lot but still
Sometimes I wish and I could have a better understanding of how you feel
Tyrone, this is hard for me
Because you're too intelligent for this
You're funny, energetic, honest, and sweet
Let's not let this be something I'll miss

I'll always love you

I'm excited about us going off to college, but I fear for our separation
The thought of you meeting someone else, the stress, the desperation
It's a new start, a new beginning, a chance to be to be experimental
A chance at life, to make a difference, working together without being judgmental
I'm going to miss you dearly and I hope for the best
You've brought excited into my life, showed me opportunity, you the very best
The time we've spent together, some great times, some not so very bad
The times we connected with those happy thoughts and the moments we shared that were sad
Going away gives me an opportunity to trust more, it gives us a chance to be free
But most of all it gives us time to pursue future goals and enjoy the finer things
Baby, this is our time to shine, it's our time to show the world what we have to offer, that's the truth
And no matter what's in store, or what happens I'll always love you

My Chocolate Thunder

The stress in my life
Has caused me a lot of pain
Worrying about things that don't matter
Has driven me insane
When things in my life go good
I can't help but wonder
What it would be like
Without Ty
My chocolate thunder

My Ultimate Goal

It's amazing to me what people would do today
How they'd do anything; rat out anybody just to get their way
Stabbing their friends in the back just for attention
They make the first punch when fighting then complain about suspension
People of the same race; who'd think they'd get along
They have disagreements like lyrics in a controversial rap song
What they talk about is the truth yet those haters put them down
And when things catch up with them they want to leave town
Not understanding why people do these things can be stressing to the soul
Because making a difference just for one simple thing would be my ultimate goal

My Own Dreams

How is it I love someone and not want to be friends?
How is it I can share everything but when it's all over just put it to an end?
How is it I feel like giving up on some of the most important moments of my life?
Just because things don't work out perfectly and other obstacles give me strife
How is it that love can hurt but it's suppose to be the key to my heart
How is it I can feel close to someone yet I can feel farther apart
How it is love can make me do some of the craziest things
How is it I have goals but don't believe in my own dreams?

What I'm Seeking

I'm so confused about how I feel for you
I like friends I want more too
I mean do I really like him or am I just looking for love
do I really like birdies or do I really like doves
That didn't have anything to do with my thoughts I just got side track
but now I'm focusing so now I'm back
I think it's just I want someone to love me
and I think that's just hard for people to see
I want someone to love me for me and to keep it real

Not a person who is of others opinions and scared to handle how they feel
I try to feel it real I try to keep being great
I try to stay committed to a r relationship but the other way around is at stake
I want someone to want to marry me and ask me to be there wife
I want someone to love me and stay in my life

I'm not into the marriage thing, but is there someone but there who loves me
maybe one person maybe two or maybe even three
No one understands my expressions for they think I'm obsessed with insanity thoughts
But it's not me whose insane about thinking its inner personality; outer thoughts
I don't care if there black, white, Mexican, or Puerto Rican
It's only love for myself from another is what I'm seekin

Credits

Jorgensen, Jon https://www.youtube.com/watch?v=zng2piCy4RA

Author

Wanda Bigler

The author, Wanda Bigler, born in STL 1990, is an author, small business owner-nonprofit, college graduate, daughter, friend, sister, wife, Christian, colleague, lover, and much more. She has other self-published books; (1) "Emotional Distress: a brief selection of poetry and (2) Paige's Testimony Part I. She has 2 older sibling brothers who have diagnosis of Autism and Schizophrenia. She uses her childhood trauma to motivate & help inspire others in the community. She graduated from Missouri State University with a Bachelor of General Studies degree. She is currently working on a Master of Social Work degree. She also has a self-starting non-profit "Cr8UrVision" that she began in April 2020 that she hopes will help others to re-invent themselves & fulfil their lives purpose or create it. In 2018, she married her best friend and wonderful husband Christopher Bigler. They currently have 2 fur children between the two.